Mighty Machines

Tanks

by Matt Doeden

Consulting Editor: Gail Saunders-Smith, PhD

Capstone
press

Mankato, Minnesota

Pebble Plus is published by Capstone Press,
151 Good Counsel Drive, P.O. Box 669, Mankato, Minnesota 56002.
www.capstonepress.com

1 2 3 4 5 6 10 09 08 07 06 05

Library of Congress Cataloging-in-Publication Data
Doeden, Matt.
   Tanks / by Matt Doeden.
   p. cm.—(Pebble plus: mighty machines)
   Includes bibliographical references and index.
   ISBN 0-7368-3659-4 (hardcover)
   ISBN 0-7368-5143-7 (paperback)
   1. Tanks (Military science)—Juvenile literature. I. Title. II. Series.
UG446.5.D62 2005
623.7'4752—dc22   2004012657

Summary: Simple text and photographs present military tanks, their parts, and their crew.

Editorial Credits
Martha E. H. Rustad, editor; Molly Nei, set designer; Kate Opseth and Ted Williams, book designer;
   Jo Miller, photo researcher; Scott Thoms, photo editor

Photo Credits
Corbis/George Hall, 20–21
Digital Vision, 1
DVIC/Chuck Croston, 17; JOSN Gael Rene, 18–19; PH1 (NAC) Stephen Batiz, 14–15;
   SPC Christina Ann Horne, 13; SPC David Faas, 10–11; Steve Catlin, cover
Fotodynamics/Ted Carlson, 4–5, 6–7, 8–9

Note to Parents and Teachers

The Mighty Machines set supports national standards related to science, technology, and society. This book describes and illustrates tanks. The images support early readers in understanding the text. The repetition of words and phrases helps early readers learn new words. This book also introduces early readers to subject-specific vocabulary words, which are defined in the Glossary section. Early readers may need assistance to read some words and to use the Table of Contents, Glossary, Read More, Internet Sites, and Index sections of the book.

Table of Contents

What Are Tanks?

Tanks are mighty fighting machines. Armies use tanks in battles.

Parts of Tanks

Tanks roll on small wheels.
Long tracks cover the wheels.
Tracks help tanks move
over rough ground.

wheel

track

Tanks are covered in armor.

This metal shell protects

the crew inside.

Tanks have big guns
called cannons. Cannons
can turn in any direction.

Tanks have machine guns.

Tank crews fire machine guns
during battles.

machine gun

Tank Crews

Commanders are in charge of tanks. They give orders to the rest of the crew.

15

Drivers steer tanks.

They sit in the front.

driver

Gunners aim at targets.

They fire the guns.

Mighty Machines

Crews drive tanks into battle.

Tanks are mighty machines.

Glossary

aim—to point a weapon at a target

armor—a tank's metal covering; armor protects a tank from bullets and bombs.

army—a group of people trained to fight on land

cannon—a large gun that fires large shells

commander—a person who leads a tank crew

crew—a team of people who work together

gunner—a crew member who shoots a tank's weapons

machine gun—a gun that can fire bullets quickly without reloading

steer—to make a vehicle go in a certain direction

target—an object at which to aim or shoot

track—a piece of metal and rubber that stretches around a tank's wheels

Read More

Budd, E. S. *Tanks.* Machines at Work. Chanhassen, Minn.: Child's World, 2002.

Cornish, Geoff. *Tanks.* Military Hardware in Action. Minneapolis: Lerner, 2003.

Internet Sites

FactHound offers a safe, fun way to find Internet sites related to this book. All of the sites on FactHound have been researched by our staff.

Here's how:

1. Visit *www.facthound.com*

2. Type in this special code **0736836594** for age-appropriate sites. Or enter a search word related to this book for a more general search.

3. Click on the **Fetch It** button.

FactHound will fetch the best sites for you!

Index

Word Count: 102
Grade: 1
Early-Intervention Level: 16